D0819740

War in the Gulf

PERSIAN GULF NATIONS

Written By: Paul J. Deegan

Published by Abdo & Daughters, 6535 Cecilia Circle, Edina, Minnesota 55439.

Library bound edition distributed by Rockbottom Books, Pentagon Tower, P.O. Box 36036, Minneapolis, Minnesota 55435.

Library of Congress Number: 91-073072   ISBN: 1-56239-029-5

Cover Photo and Page 5 Photo by: Margaret Coleman Abdo
Inside Photos by: Pictorial Parade: 7, 13, 15, 22, 24, 26, 30, 39, 43, 49, 52,
                                         63
                Globe Photos: 11, 17, 18, 21, 33, 37, 41, 46, 47, 55, 57, 60
                The Granger Collection: 28

Edited by: Rosemary Wallner

TABLE OF CONTENTS

THE MIDDLE EASTERN COUNTRIES

The Persian Gulf washes the shores of eight Middle Eastern countries. Two of the first great civilizations developed over 5,000 years ago in this region. However, the Middle East was an area unfamiliar to most Americans when the Persian Gulf crisis began in the summer of 1990.

Scholars differ on which countries make up the Middle East. Many believe it includes Israel, Iran, Iraq, Jordan, Kuwait, Saudia Arabia, Syria, and Turkey as well as, the former Arab sheikdoms and onetime British Protectorates at the south and southeastern edges of the Arabian peninsula — today the countries of Yemen, Oman, the United Arab Emirates, Qatar, and Bahrain. Also included are Egypt, the Sudan, and the island nation of Cyprus off the southern coast of Turkey and west of Syria.

All the countries of the Middle East are on the Asian continent except for Egypt and the Sudan. Egypt is in northeast Africa, west of Israel, and Sudan is directly south of Egypt.

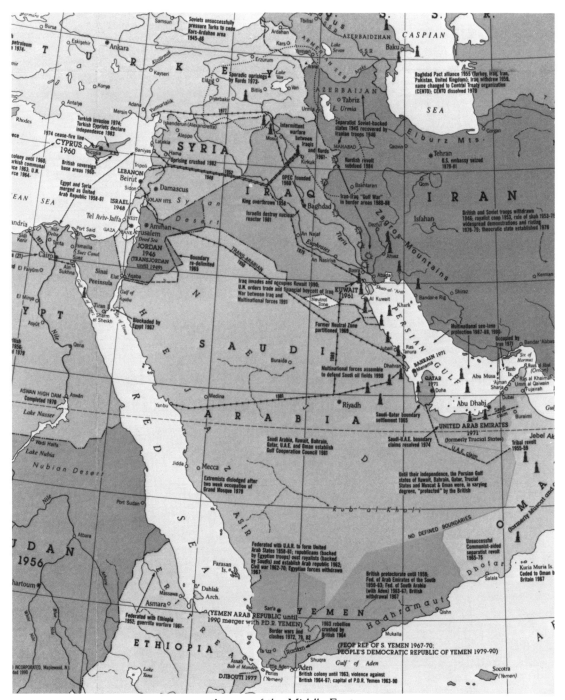

A map of the Middle East.

The bodies of water off the northwestern part of Turkey divide Asia and Europe. The Red Sea and the Gulf of Suez separate Asia and Africa.

Iran, Iraq, Jordan, Kuwait, Saudi Arabia, and Turkey are the subjects of this book. Israel and the Palestinians and Lebanon and Syria are the subjects of another book, *The Arab-Israeli Conflict, In The Persian Gulf War* series.

ANCIENT BUT LITTLE KNOWN

Actually, the Middle East was unfamiliar to most of the world before the second decade of this century even though the region's history dates to antiquity.

The civilizations of Sumer and Egypt developed in the Middle East after 3,500 B.C. Iraq is the site of the ancient kingdom of Sumer. The kingdom of Babylon was also in Iraq.

Great cities of the Middle East include the capitals of modern Iraq and Syria, Baghdad and Damascus.

The city of Damascus.

Baghdad was designed in the eighth century by a Moslem ruler. Arabs had come to the area in the seventh century, but Jews had been living there 1,300 hundred years earlier. Thus Baghdad has been described as "one of the two great Jewish cities of Asia (along with Jerusalem)."

Damascus, Syria, has been called "an important city for all historical ages." It is believed to be the oldest continuously lived-in urban center in the world. Its beginnings, a historian says, are "lost in the mists of time." However, it was an oasis town "before there were Jews or Arabs, Moslems or Christians . . . " Persia — today's Iran — was a powerful empire 2,500 years ago.

The area once known as Palestine is the biblical homeland of the Hebrews, the Jewish people. In addition to Judaism, the Middle East is the birthplace of two of the world's other major religions — Christianity and Islam, whose followers are called Moslems. It is believed Christ lived in Palestine and Mohammed, founder of Islam, lived in what is today Saudi Arabia.

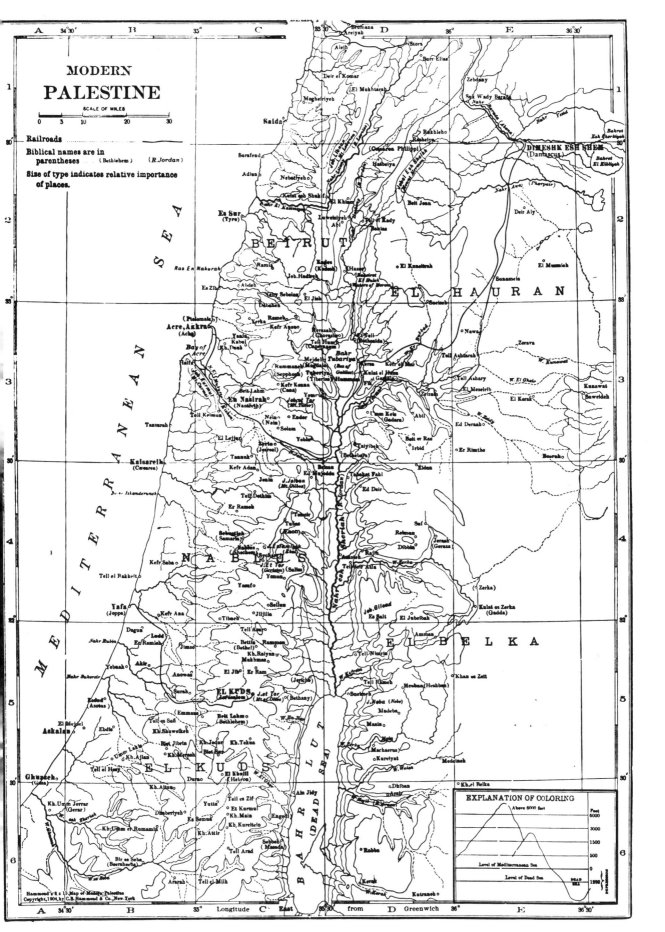

MODERN
PALESTINE

SCALE OF MILES

Railroads ....

Biblical names are in
  parentheses (Bethlehem) (R.Jordan)

Size of type indicates relative importance
  of places.

EXPLANATION OF COLORING

Above 6000 feet

	Feet
	6000
	3000
	1500
	500
Level of Mediterranean Sea	0
Level of Dead Sea	DEAD SEA 1292

Hammond's 8 x 11 Map of Modern Palestine
Copyright, 1904, by C.S. Hammond & Co., New York.

Longitude East from Greenwich

GULF WAR FOCUSES
ATTENTION ON MIDDLE EAST

When Iraq invaded one of the Middle East's smallest nations, Kuwait, on August 2, 1990, the United States reacted by placing several hundred thousand armed forces in Saudi Arabia. Operation Desert Shield put the Middle East in the headlines day after day.

The region's countries remained on the front pages of American newspapers as fighting began in January 1991 and Operation Desert Shield became Operation Desert Storm. Events in the war's aftermath kept the region in the news well into the spring of 1991.

Iraq, the United States' enemy in the Gulf War is bordered not only by Kuwait on the south, but by five other Middle Eastern nations — Saudi Arabia, also to the south; Syria and Jordan to the west; Turkey to the north; and Iran to the east. The Shatt al Arab waterway, a gateway to the Persian Gulf is on the Iraq-Iran border.

Lebanon is on Syria's southwest border.

Lebanon's southern neighbor is Israel, which
borders Syria and Jordan to the east and Egypt's
Sinai Peninsula on the west. Syria and Jordan
share a southern and northern border,
respectively.

U.S. forces begin the buildup in Saudi Arabia.

ISLAM DOMINATES REGION

Although the Middle East is a complex region with competing cultures and sometimes opposing political systems, Islam is dominant. It usually is the basis of political life. As a historian noted, "most residents of the Middle East have for over a thousand years avowed faith in a Holy Law that governs all of life, including government and politics."

The strong belief in the West in a secular civil government, he says, "is an alien creed" in the Middle East.

Israel, a Jewish nation, and Lebanon, where Christians have played a major political role, are exceptions to the dominance of Islam. Moslems, however, strengthened their political role in Lebanon as the 1990s began.

Islam — the word means "submission to God" in Arabic — was founded by an Arab prophet, Mohammed. Followers of Islam are called Moslems ("submitters" to God). Mohammed lived in what is today Saudi Arabia and where he was born in about A.D. 575 and died in 632. His tribe had been desert nomads, but he was born in Mecca, a trade center despite its location in a hot and barren valley.

Five times a day, Moslems show their devotion to Allah by bowing to the East.

Mecca is in the long, narrow, mountainous western section of the Arabian peninsula known as the Hejaz. The Hejaz is some 750 miles long and about 200 miles at its widest point.

Opponents of his religious teaching forced Mohammed to flee to Medina, 300 miles northwest of Mecca, in 622. Eight years later, Mohammed's armed followers captured Mecca. These two cities are Islam's holiest shrines.

Mohammed thought that there was one God — Allah — and that Allah created the world and governs it. Moslems believe in the creed that there is no God but Allah and Mohammed is His prophet.

For Moslems there are five compulsory daily prayers at dawn, midday, the middle of the afternoon, sunset and after nightfall. In Moslem regions, everything comes to a stop at these times when the call to prayer is made from a tower which is part of a mosque, the Moslem place of public worship.

Every healthy Moslem must make a pilgrimmage to Mecca once in a lifetime.

Every Moslem must make a journey to Mecca at least once in their life time.

The Koran ("something read"), composed of
Mohammed's revelations, is Islam's sacred book.
Moslems consider its contents the words of God.
When you read the Koran, they say, Allah talks to
you. Moslems try to live by the Koran and, in
Islam, religion is woven into every part of life.
Islamic law provides for each specific situation.

ARAB AND MOSLEM NOT SAME

Most Arabs are Moslems and Arabic is the common language in the Middle East. However, only 15 percent of all Moslems are Arabs.

In the Middle East, for example, Egyptians, Iranians, Kurds, Turks, and Syrians are peoples from different ethnic backgrounds who are Moslems.

And not all Arabs are Moslems. Some five percent of Arabs are Christians and there are Arab Jews.

Worldwide, an estimated 20 percent of the people are Moslems, second to Christians' 33 percent. Most Moslems are Asians. Islam is diverse and embraces cultural and political differences as well as differing opinions about Islam itself. The vast majority of Moslems, some say 90 percent, are Sunni Moslems, one of about 70 sects in Islam.

Sunnis follow custom, Mohammed's way of doing things, and rely on community. They trace their descent to Mohammed's tribe. Sunni rulers are held to be the secular and spiritual successor to Mohammed.

Sunni Moslems follow certain customs and tradition: one custom is to touch the black stone.

The other well-known sect is the Shiite Moslems who take their name from the Arab word "shia," meaning party. Shiites believe that Mohammed's cousin and son-in-law, Ali, was his lawful successor. They believe God has chosen a series of "imams," religious leaders, descending from Ali, to lead the Islamic community.

Another sect within Sunni Islam is the Wahhabis, who are dominant today in the land of Mohammed's birth.

Istanbul, Turkey, the land of the Ottoman Empire.

PERSIAN GULF NATIONS —
A PRODUCT OF WORLD WAR I

Today's Middle Eastern countries, most of them Moslem-dominated, were formed after the first world war was fought between 1914 and 1918. World War I began on July 28, 1914, when the Hapsburg Empire — Austria and Hungary — invaded Serbia (today a republic of Yugoslavia). The far-ranging war ended late in 1918 Germany surrendering and signing an armistice on November 11, 1918. At least 10 million peole were killed or missing during the war.

Germany and the Ottoman Empire (Turkey) joined with the Hapsburg Empire as the Central Powers in what was to be the losing side in the war. Bulgaria joined them in 1915.

Britain and France immediately sided with Serbia. Belgium and Russia were soon fighting back against the Central Powers. Altogether, over 20 countries eventually joined the war on the Allied side, although not all of them provided soldiers. The British forces included troops from the dominion nations of the British Empire including Australia, Canada, India, and New Zealand. The United States did not enter the conflict until declaring war on Germany on April 6, 1917.

Britain and France were on the victorious Allied side in World War I. The background of how the Middle East was reconstructed after the war is extensive and complicated. However, essentially what happened is that Britain and France carved up the Arabic-speaking countries of the Middle East. Britain and France wanted to divide the territory gained in the war in a way that best would suit their interests as they identified them at that time.

One historian said, ". . . Britain drew the map of the Arab world after World War I." Another says Iraq and Jordan "were British inventions, lines drawn on an empty map after (the war.)" France drew the dividing lines between Moslems and Christians in the Syria-Lebanon region. The new nations did not reflect history nor take into account ethnic, tribal, language, or religious differences. The new boundaries in the Middle East were "artificially imposed from above," said one expert on the region.

The European powers also created what today are Saudi Arabia and the other nations of the Arabian Peninsula including Kuwait. Also involved in the postwar politics were Iran and Turkey.

20

So was Egypt, which had been ruled by Britain for decades and was a British protectorate at the end of the war.

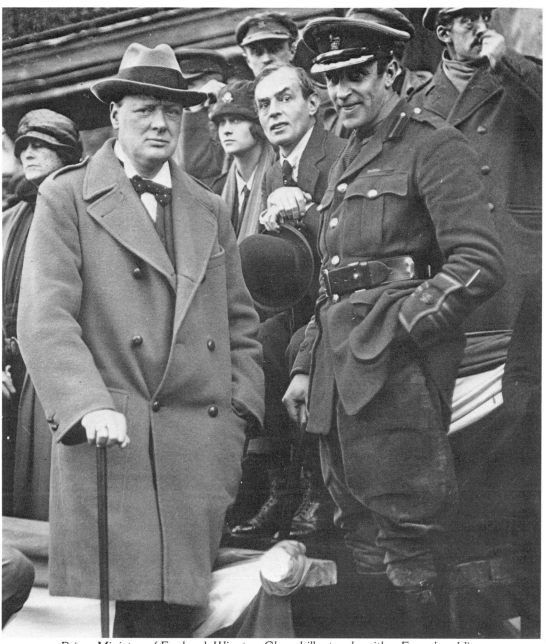

Prime Minister of England, Winston Churchill, stands with a French soldier. Britain and France were victorious Allies during World War I.

The Ottoman Empire was a major world power for centuries. This Mosque was at the heart of its power structure in Istanbul, Turkey.

WAR ENDS OTTOMAN EMPIRE

Prior to World War I, most of the Middle East was part of the Ottoman Empire. A specific aim of Britain's participation in the war was the destruction of that empire. Europeans assumed that defeating the empire would give the victor control of the region. Britain, in particular, wanted to emerge from the war with it's far-flung domain intact. France had an interest in Syria, including its Mount Lebanon coast, from the time its knights had built castles there during the Crusades a thousand years earlier.

The Ottoman Empire had been a major world power for centuries. Centered in Constantinople (formerly known as Byzantium and now Istanbul, Turkey). At its height in the 16th century, the Ottoman Empire extended from today's Russia south to the coasts of Arabia and the Persian Gulf and into North Africa. Much of Europe also was part of the empire which once ruled over 20 different nationalities.

Though it's Turkish-speaking leaders, descendants of an Asian people, ruled from Constantinople, the Ottoman Empire was a Moslem not a Turkish state.

Most of the people living in the empire were Moslems. The Ottoman Sultan was held by Sunni Moslems to be the caliph or successor to Mohammed.

When World War I ended in 1918, the British had achieved their goal of finishing off the Ottoman Empire.

The Ottoman Empire was defeated by the British during World War I.

THE ARABS AND THE WAR

Hidden away in western Arabia at the time of World War I was Hussein ibn Ali. Hussein (no relation to today's Iraqi president, Saddam Hussein) was the Emir (ruler) of Mecca in the Hejaz region. Hussein was also called Sherif Hussein. A "sherif" is an important person who is a descendant of Mohammed. Sherif Hussein was the guardian of the Moslem holy places of Mecca and Medina where non-Moslems were forbidden to enter.

Mecca then was still in the region of Arabia which was part of the Ottoman Empire. For Moslem pilgrims making the journey to Mecca, it was a two-day camel ride over the desolate Arabian landscape from Jidda. The Hejazi port city on the Red Sea, Jidda, about 45 miles to the west, is today a city of some 560,000. A major task of the local representative of the Ottoman government was to prevent Bedouin tribes from robbing the pilgrims.

For Moslem pilgrims making the journey to Mecca, it was a two day camel ride over the desolate Arabian desert.

After the world war began, Hussein took care not to offend either side. Eventually, however, he decided the Turks were going to remove him if they could. So in June 1916 he "proclaimed a rebellion against the Ottoman Empire." The British navy backed this move by putting some ships along the Hejaz coastline.

There never really was rebellion because other Arabs did not join Hussein's tribal followers. But almost a year later, in the spring of 1917, T.E. Lawrence, a British government official and army officer who became known as "Lawrence of Arabia," went into the Arabian desert with troops of a northern Arabian Bedouin leader.

These fighters moved north and in early July captured Aqaba (today part of Jordan), a seaport at the southern tip of the region then known as Palestine. Aquaba is on a channel of the Red Sea.

The British wanted to control Palestine, a land bridge from British-controlled Egypt to India, where Britain also was dominant. Whoever controlled Palestine might also block the Suez Canal, thus threatening the sea route from west to east as well.

T.E. Lawrence, a British army officer during World War I, became known as the famous "Lawrence of Arabia."

In the autumn of 1917 the British invaded Palestine, held by Turkish troops commanded by German officers. The British forces were supported by some 1,000 Bedouin troops headed by Sherif Hussein's son, Feisal. The troops from the Hejaz were fighting under a flag designed for them by the British. Its black, white, green and red colors "were meant to symbolize the past glory of Moslem Arab empires," says a historian.

The British captured Jerusalem in December; Feisal's troops then moved into Transjordan, the name given by the Romans to this area because it is "trans" (across) the River Jordan from Palestine.

Feisal's Arab troops also fought in the British campaign in Syria, and when the war ended, Feisal, at least in name, ruled Syria with the support of the British. Later, France would stake its longtime claim to Syria.

Just as they had put Feisal in power in Iraq, British officials in 1921 chose Feisal's brother, Abdullah, to be the temporary governor of Transjordan. Abdullah is the grandfather of the country's present ruler, King Hussein. (No relataion of Saddam Hussein.)

Winston Churchill, Britain's Colonial Secretary in 1921, intended that Abdullah would remain in Transjordan for only a few months. But it didn't turn out that way.

The British captured the Holy City of Jerusalem during World War I. Today Jerusalem is under Jewish Jurisdiction.

The British also knew the decision to award Transjordan to the Arabia-based House of Hashem would upset the Hashemites' Arabian rival, the House of Saud. The rivalry was rooted in religion. Hashemites are Sunni Moslems. The Saudis, too, were Moslems but were stern religious moralists, called Wahhabis. Both the Hashemites and the Saudis wanted to control Arabia.

The British tried to pacify the Saudi leader, Abdul Aziz, also known as Ibn Saud, by increasing the annual subsidy they paid to him. However, this gesture was not enough to keep Britain from becoming entangled in the conflict between the two Arabian powers. About a year later, a few thousand Saudi horsemen rode across the desert to attack Abdullah. British armed forces turned them back as they neared Amman, now the capital city of Jordan.

At the end of 1922, Britain also forced upon Ibn Saud an agreement which defined the Saudi kingdom's borders with both Iraq and Kuwait. The boundaries were drawn by a British civil servant.

That same year the League of Nations made Britain the trustee of Palestine. Britain's mission under the Palestine Mandate was to create a Jewish national homeland in Palestine while also protecting the rights of the Palestinian Arabs.

However, Churchill's decision to put Abdullah in Transjordan eventually meant that the future Jewish homeland would not include the land east of the Jordan River. Churchill's decision, in fact, had put three-fourths of the land area of Palestine under the rule of an Arab. This happened despite support in Britain for establishing a Jewish homeland in Palestine.

Abdullah's stay in Transjordan became permanent and today few even recall that Jordan was once the largest part of Palestine.

IRAN

The Islamic Republic of Iran, once called Persia, is one of the world's oldest countries. Its history dates back almost 5,000 years.

Winston Churchill, Prime Minister of England during World War I.

Iran is located north and northeast of the Persian Gulf. Iran borders Iraq on the west, the Soviet Union on the north and Afghanistan and Pakistan on the east. Iran is the second largest Middle Eastern country in land size although 70 percent of Iran's 635,000 square miles are mountains and vast deserts where no one lives.

Although it is a Moslem country because Moslem Arabs conquered it in the seventh century, Iranians are not Arabs. Two-thirds of them are descendents of people from central Asia, called Aryans, who established the Persian Empire. At its peak in 500 B.C., the Persian Empire ruled most of southwest Asia and parts of Europe and Africa.

As rival dynasties moved in and out of the area conquering the empire's warriors, Persia's boundaries were gradually restricted to what they are today. As part of the Ottoman Empire during World War I, Persia was a battlefield. After that war, the country was a constitutional monarchy ruled by shahs (kings). It became officially known as Iran in 1935.

Iran became an Islamic republic in 1979 after Ayatollah Ruhollah Khomeini, a Shiite religious leader, led a revolution that overthrew the ruling shah. On April 4, 1979, militant revolutionaries captured 52 Americans in a raid on the United States Embassy in Tehran and held them captive for 444 days.

Islam is the state religion. Ninety-eight percent of the estimated 54 million Iranians are Moslems, 90 percent of them Shiite. Iran's official language is Persian, also called Farsi.

The nation's supreme leader, Seyed Ali Khamenei, was elected by Moslem clerics in June 1989 after Khomeini's death. The nation's president is Hashemi Rafsanjani.

Iran was frequently in the news during its 1980-1988 war with Iraq. Iran stayed neutral in the Gulf War, but worked with the United States and its allies against Iraq.

Oil, discovered in the early 1900s, has been a great source of wealth for Iran. With Iraq's oil industry crippled after the Gulf War, Iran was the second largest producer of crude oil in the Middle East after Saudi Arabia. The United States lifted a ban on importing Iranian oil in June 1991.

IRAQ

Iraq was long known as Mesopotamia. It is west of Iran and north of Saudia Arabia.

Five centuries of Ottoman rule of Mesopotamia had ended in 1917 when Britain's Anglo-Indian Army captured the country. The city of Baghdad fell on March 11, 1917. The British began using the Arab term, Iraq, for the country, and controlled it until 1920 when it was placed under a League of Nations mandate they were to administer.

The British had not forgotten their ally from the Hejaz, Feisal. They gave Iraq to him in 1921, installing him as king under the League of Nations mandate. Britain had combined Sunni and Shiite Moslem, Jewish, and Kurdish populations to form a new country.

The Kurds are a non-Arab tribal people. They were scattered among the plateaus and mountains in the area where today the borders of Iraq, Iran, Turkey, Syria, and the Soviet Republic of Armenia overlap. Mostly Sunni Moslems, the Kurds numbered some two and a half million in 1921.

*The city of Baghdad, Iraq, fell to the British in World War I; this is the
Presidential Palace in Baghdad prior to Operation Desert Storm.*

The Kurds had quarreled with neighboring Arabs and Armenians through the years. They fought against British attempts to organize them in 1919. Under a 1920 treaty between Britain and France and the Ottoman Sultan, the area known as Kurdistan was granted autonomy.

But in 1921 there was disagreement among British officials about what to do with the Kurds. Some wanted them to become part of the new kingdom in Baghdad. Others favored an independent Kurdistan. It was decided at a meeting of British officials in Cairo, Egypt, that the Kurds would form a separate unit and be governed by the British official for Iraq. The effect was that the Kurdistan region was left out when the former Ottoman territories were partitioned.

So yet today an estimated seven million Kurds remain a nation without a homeland.

During the summer of 1921, the Council of Ministers, the official rulers in Baghdad, declared Feisal to be the country's constitutional monarch. Iraq replaced Mesopotamia as the name of Feisal's new kingdom.

Feisal II (left), the former king of Iraq, is in a long line of Feisal's to succeed to the throne.

Iraq was granted some independence under a 1922 treaty with Britain. But the country's political leaders continued to press for statehood. Iraq gained its independence in 1932 under King Feisal when Britain's mandate ended. A year later, the king died at 56. He was succeeded by his son, Ghazi, who died in an auto accident six years later. The new king was Ghazi's young son, Feisal II. He was assassinated in 1958 after the Baath Party, whose members included the then 21-year-old Saddam Hussein, helped overthrow his dynasty.

The official ruling body under the Baathists was the National Council for Revolutionary Command. This was the forerunner to the National Command Council often referenced during the Persian Gulf War.

The Baathists were in and out of power until 1968 when they seized the control they still hold. Since 1979, Saddam has been president of the Republic of Iraq, a country tightly controlled by Saddam and the Baath Party.

Oil wealth fueled the military buildup in Iraq which climaxed in the Persian Gulf War. The oil industry was nationalized in 1972.

21-year-old Saddam Hussein helped to overthrow King Feisal's reign. This is a present day photo of Saddam Hussein.

Eight years later, in September 1980, Iraq attacked Iran over a longtime dispute about the control of the Shatt al Arab waterway. This conflict ended with a 1988 cease-fire.

Iraq was a nation of some 18 million people at the time of the Persian Gulf War. Most of the population lived along the historic Tigris and Euphrates Rivers or in the fertile plain between them. West of the Euphrates, the country is an arid desert. Only one-third of the nation's land can be farmed.

Eighty percent of the Iraqi people are Arabs and 15 percent are Kurds. Ninety-five percent of Iraq's population is Moslem. Although Sunni Moslems control the Baath Party and dominate the government, Shiite Moslems make up 60 percent of the population. The Shiites, who have lacked influence in Iraq despite their numbers, are the majority group in southern Iraq where they consider Majas a holy city.

In June 1991 Iraq was trying to recover from the military pounding it had taken during its decisive defeat by the United States-led coalition in the Persian Gulf War.

A burning oil field in Kuwait.

Five months after Iraq invaded and took over Kuwait in August 1990, the forces of Operation Desert Storm attacked Iraqi troops in Kuwait and bombed Iraq itself. The Iraqi soldiers were driven out of Kuwait and pursued into Iraq by coalition troops before a cease-fire agreement was reached after the fighting was halted on February 27, 1991. The bombing destroyed Iraq's infrastructure and raised the possibility of serious health problems.

Following the cease-fire, the Kurds rebelled against Baghdad as did the Shiite majority in southern Iraq. The Kurds were again seeking an independent homeland.

JORDAN

Jordan, formerly named Transjordan, is on the southwest edge of Iraq and the northwest edge of Saudi Arabia. It includes the major portion of the region once known as Palestine.

Seventy years after Britain installed Abdullah as its ruler, Jordan remains an Arab kingdom, the Hashemite Kingdom of Jordan. It and Saudi Arabia are the only countries named for families.

Jordan is a constitutional monarchy and has been ruled for nearly 40 years by King Hussein. His grandfather, Abdullah, was assassinated in 1951 by a Palestinian. King Hussein was only 18 when he succeeded his mentally ill father a year later. It has been an uneasy rule. King Hussein has survived several assassination attempts.

Transjordan, as it was still known then, was granted complete independence from Britain in 1946. Three years later it was named the Hashemite Kingdom of Jordan. Political parties were banned in Jordan in 1957, but in June 1991 an agreement was reached between the king and major politicians to revive multiparty democracy in the kingdom.

Jordan is mostly a desert of 37,300 square miles. Four million people, the majority now Palestinians, live in Jordan. Ninety-three percent of the population are Moslems. One million of them live in the 3,300 square miles which make up the West Bank, the land west of the River Jordan. King Hussein had annexed the territory in 1950, but Israel has occupied it since the Arab-Israeli War of 1967.

Jordan's King Hussein.

46

For a long time he was the Arab leader on the best terms with the United States, King Hussein found himself in a very awkward position during the Persian Gulf War. He is a non-Palestinian running a country which has had a Palestinian majority since an earlier Arab-Israeli war in 1948. Jordan is a poor nation and has no oil. It was economically dependent upon Iraq. Before Operation Desert Shield, 90 percent of Jordan's oil, and 40 percent of its goods and services depended upon trade with Iraq and Kuwait. So King Hussein tried not to take sides in the Gulf War.

U.S. troops gearing up for Operation Desert Storm.

KUWAIT

The tiny state of Kuwait, located on the northwest edge of the Persian Gulf, is smaller than the state of New Jersey. It is swallowed geographically by Iraq to the north and Saudi Arabia to the south. At its widest point, Kuwait is only 95 miles from its eastern to its western border. It measures 90 miles north to south. Kuwait is a desert with no rivers or lakes. Its 6,900 square miles include nine offshore islands.

Kuwait began as a trading post at what is now Kuwait City when Bedouin tribes migrated from the Nejd Desert in central Arabia to the coast in the early 1700s. The tribes chose the Sabah family to administer their settlement. Since that time Sabah family members have run government activities as their personal affairs.

Kuwait has been under British protection since 1899 when the Sabahs made a treaty with Britain to protect them from their neighbors.

The oil boom after World War II changed life in Kuwait. Before 1946 it was one of the world's poorer nations. Then it became a major exporter of oil.

Bedouin tribesmen, people who live in the Nejd Desert of central Arabia.

49

Drilling had actually begun in 1936 after a joint American-British company had been granted the concession to do so in 1934. By the 1950s, oil wealth dominated the Kuwaiti economy.

The state of Kuwait is a kingdom headed by an emir from the ruling al Sabah family. Sheik Jaber al Ahmad al Sabah became the 13th Emir of Kuwait in 1977. The 1,000-member Sabah family has ruled Kuwait since 1756. Islam is the state religion. Islam allows a man to have more than one wife and the present emir has four wives and 40 children.

The Sabahs indirectly control Kuwait's huge oil wealth and they have created a prosperous welfare state. Kuwait City, still a town of mud huts in the early 1950s, was built into a modern city including skyscrapers.

The Kuwaiti government estimated that 2.2 million people were living in Kuwait at the begining of August 1990. Only 700,000, about 28 percent, were Kuwaitis. Most of the Kuwaitis were Sunni Moslems. But Shiites constituted a large underclass, numbering about one-third of the Kuwaitis. A few Shiites were members of rich merchant families. Most were Iranian origin.

Fewer than 10 percent of the Kuwaitis, some 62,000 men, were eligible to vote, if there had been elections. Voting was restricted to men over 21 who could read and write and who could trace their origin to families in Kuwait before 1920. However, the emir had suspended the 1962 Kuwaiti constitution in 1986.

In pre-war Kuwait, nearly all the work was done by foreigners. The government was the largest employer of Kuwaitis. The foreign workers included Palestinians, Egyptians, and Jordanians. More recently, there were Pakistanis, Filipinos, Indians, Bangladeshis, and Sri Lankans. Foreigners did almost all the labor but they also held about 80 percent of the managerial and professional jobs.

Kuwait was virtually destroyed by the occupying Iraqi troops during the Gulf conflict. As the summer of 1991 approached, skies were still blackened by smoke from burning Kuwaiti oil wells, set on fire by retreating Iraqi troops. Ironically, Kuwait had spent billions of dollars aiding Iraq in its war with Iran during the 1980s. (Saudi Arabia also had helped Iraq pay for the war with Iran.)

After the Persian Gulf War, Americans, mostly Army civil affairs troops, actually administered most of Kuwait. There was a tremendous amount of rebuilding to do, but Kuwait's oil riches gave it the financial means to reconstruct the country. It would be some time, however, before the vast damage to the oil industry was repaired.

SAUDI ARABIA

The Kingdom of Saudi Arabia occupies most of the Arabian peninsula. The Persian Gulf borders the kingdom on the east, the Red Sea on the west and Iraq is on its northeastern border.

One-fourth the size of the United States, Saudi Arabia is basically an arid desert — dry, barren land. Only one percent of the land is used for crops. As in neighboring Kuwait, there are no natural bodies of water. A sandy desert in the south, almost as large as the state of Texas, is uninhabited but takes up 250,000 of the kingdom's total 830,000 square miles.

Water is one of the Middle East's scarcest assets and is a particular problem in Saudi Arabia and Kuwait. These two countries must desalt sea water to obtain all their fresh water and to meet their industrial needs.

Burning oil fields of Kuwait. It will be very expensive and take a lot of time before the damage to Kuwaits oil fields can be repaired.

Saudi Arabia was formed in this century as the result of conquest. In 1902 Abdul Aziz, also known as Ibn Saud led a military raid from Kuwait on the Rashidi dynasty and captured Riyadh in central Arabia. The Saud clan had once ruled much of Arabia, but had been defeated and had taken refuge in Kuwait. The warrior Ibn Saud set out to reconquer the lost territory.

Ibn Saud also was the leader of the Wahhabi sect of Sunni Islam, which he had revived. In 1912, the rebirth of Wahhabism brought about a warrior brotherhood, the Ikhwan (brethren).

Ibn Saud's warriors eventually put together a kingdom which today embraces 88 major desert tribes. The powerful warlord eventually took the eastern region of Arabia and the Hejaz area in the west, the home of his archrival, Sherif Hussein. The last area to fall to the fierce Ikhwan was the mountainous land even further west along the Red Sea.

Today, Ibn Saud's son, King Fahd rules the Kingdom of Saudi Arabia. The kingdom includes the Moslem holy cities of Mecca and Medina. The Saudi government says the country's population is 14 and a half million. Over four million are foreigners.

King Fahd rules the Kingdom of Saudi Arabia.

Whatever their actual number, the residents live in what is described as one of the world's most conservative societies.

The kingdom is a monarchy based on the laws of Islam as interpreted by the very strict religious beliefs of the Wahhabis. The practice of any religion other than Islam is forbidden. When American soldiers came to Saudi Arabia in 1990, they entered a country that had restricted visits of journalists and usually had forbidden entrance to Jews.

The Saudi king holds power in civil and religious affairs. There is no written constitution. There are no elected officials. The House of Saud, which includes 5,000 princes, controls the country.

King Fahd is one of Ibn Saud's 43 sons by many wives, 300 by one estimate. The king has several official residences including the palace in Riyadh, the capital and largest city.

All Saudis are Moslems. Some 85 percent are Sunni, most of them Wahhabis. The rest of the Moslems are Shiite. Islamic law regulates most public affairs and dominates personal life. Justice is meted out according to strict Islamic law. Murderers and other criminal are beheaded and thieves' hands are chopped off in city squares. There also are public whippings.

Moslem society is very conservative. Women cannot drive nor travel alone. They must wear black cloaks and veils in public at all times.

Saudis are forbidden to see movies, dance, use liquor, or gamble. Videos and books and other print material are heavily censored. Women cannot drive nor may they travel alone. Their clothing must cover most of their bodies. They wear black cloaks and veils in public. Boys and girls attend separate schools. Western clothes are forbidden. Men wear cotton kerchiefs over their heads, tying them in place with a black cord.

Like Kuwait, Saudi Arabia was a very poor nation before it was discovered that immense pools of oil lay beneath its sand. One-quarter of the world's known oil reserves lie in the kingdom. Yet, when Ibn Saud died in 1953, he was still living in a mud-walled palace in Riyadh.

Large-scale production, which would make Saudi Arabia the world's largest petroleum exporter, did not begin until after World War II although Standard Oil of California had been given the oil concession in 1933 and a major deposit was found five years later. When the oil money did start coming, it went directly into the king's treasury. Oil revenue in 1990 was expected to be more than $60 billion.

As did the Sabahs in Kuwait, the ruling Saud clan has modernized Saudi Arabia and created comfortable living conditions for its subjects. The government built roads, schools, and modern hospitals. Free education and medical care is provided, and each Saudi family is given free land and an interest-free loan to build a house. There are no taxes.

In the late summer of 1990, the threat of attack by Iraq, which had invaded Kuwait, frightened the Saud family enough for them to risk stationing non-Moslem forces in Saudia Arabia.

Soon hundreds of thousands of Operation Desert Shield forces moved into northeastern Saudi Arabia. United States and coalition forces prepared themselves to eventually fight in Kuwait and Iraq in Operation Desert Storm. The Command Center of the United States military forces was located in Riyadh.

The presence of Western military forces in Saudi Arabia during the Gulf War briefly opened a closed society to outside inspection.

The U.S. forces began to prepare for the battle in Kuwait against the Iraqi army.

TURKEY

The Republic of Turkey is the northernmost of the Middle Eastern countries. The Mediterranean Sea is on its south, the Black Sea on its north. It's southern neighbors are Iraq and Syria. It shares a western border with Iran and the Soviet Union.

The terms ending World War I had allowed Ottoman authorities to remain in charge of the Turkish-speaking parts of what had been the Ottoman Empire. Mehmed VI was the last Sultan. He became Sultan in June 1918, dissolved the Turkish Parliament, and ruled by decree.

In 1921 Turkish Nationalists, who favored a Turkish-Moslem state, won a war of independence. Then a series of agreements, almost all of them finalized in 1922, divided the former Ottoman Empire between Britain, France, and Turkey.

In November 1922, a new Turkish Parliament, formed after the civil war and controlled by the Nationalists, deposed Sultan Mehmed VI. Nearly 500 years of Ottoman rule in the Middle East was over.

The Turkish National Assembly then established a Turkish national state which was the territory ruled by the Ottomans after the war.

Turkey includes 300,000 square miles, most of which are in Asia. Much of this land is rocky and barren. A small area in the northwest forms a peninsula to the European continent. This area includes the city of Istanbul.

Ninety percent of Turkey's population of some 57 million are Turks. Two million Kurds are the largest minority. Ninety-eight percent of the population is Moslem, though Islam has not been the state religion since 1928.

Twice since 1922, the government of Turkey has been overthrown. Today, the Republic of Turkey, operates under a constitution approved in national voting in November 1982. Its president, elected by a 325-member Parliament, is Turgut Ozal, who founded the Motherland Party in 1983 and led it to power.

This conservative Moslem nation traditionally has distrusted the West. However, during the Persian Gulf War, Turkey supported the United States. Ozal defied his military and many government officials in taking this stand.

Iraq had provided Turkey with $7 billion in trade before the war. The Gulf states pledged to make up half of this, but Turkey had received only half of the amount by the summer of 1991.

Istanbul, former capital of the Ottoman Empire.

GLOSSARY

ANTIQUITY: Ancient times.

ASSASSINATED: Murdered.

AUTONOMY: Having self-government.

CONCESSION: Privilege of doing busines.

CONSTITUTIONAL: Operating under a system of laws.

CREED: Formal statement of religious belief.

DEMOCRACY: Government by the people directly or through elected representatives.

DESCENDANTS: People coming from other peoples.

DESOLATE: No one lives there.

DOMINION: Under the control or influence of another nation.

DYNASTY(IES): Succeeding rulers from the same family.

EXPORTER: Selling abroad.

MINORITY: A smaller group within a larger one.

MONARCHY: Government by one ruler such as a king.

MORALIST(S): Someone who follows a system of right and wrong.

NATIONALIZE(D): Change from private to government ownership.

NOMADS: People who have no permanent home and move from place to place.

OASIS: A place in the desert where the presence of water enables grass and plants to grow.

PENINSULA: Land projecting into water.

PROTECTORATE(S): A country or region protected and to some extent controlled by a stronger nation.

REPUBLIC: A system of government where the head of state is not a king and is usually a president.

SECT(S): A group forming a unit within a larger group on the basis of a difference in belief.

SHEIKDOM(S): A region or nation ruled by an Arab leader.

UNDERCLASS: The lowest group in a society.

UNINHABITED: No one lives there.